SAMANTHA TERRELL

ON THE WING

MORE POETRY FROM JANE'S STUDIO PRESS

KEEPING AFLOAT
BY SAMANTHA TERRELL

WONDERLAND IN ALICE
PLUS OTHER WAYS OF SEEING
BY PAUL BROOKES

TIGER LILY
BY SUSAN RICHARDSON

OTHERNESSES
BY PAUL BROOKES

THE BREADCRUMB TRAIL
BY LAWRENCE MOORE

ON THE WING
A POETRY COLLECTION

JC STUDIO PRESS
Design by Jane Cornwell
www.janecornwell.co.uk

ISBN: 978-1-7384960-7-5
Also available in Ebook format.

FOREWORD

'All may be lost to time tomorrow,
but today owns every joy and sorrow'

Samantha Terrell's *On the Wing* is a murmuration of poems, each
a beautiful creature in its own right, yet each a melodious piece of
something grander.

A cyclical collection, it takes the reader on a winged journey over four
seasons, all the while encouraging them to witness the world through a
child's, or perhaps more accurately, a bird's eyes.

This sense of innocent absorption is palpable from the get-go with
Reverie in all its bead stringing, music savouring, dragonfly studying joy.
Following on, *A Day* sings an achingly poetic call to the present tense;
not the last such appeal to be found within these pages.

'Shots from arrows pointed purposefully at hearts,
sometimes, get blocked.'

We are led through the advent of spring by a series of affectionate avian
odes, before we arrive at *A Storm Called Cupid*, a tale which manages,
even as it initially talks of love's aim gone wrong, to offer comfort in
light of the strength and assuredness of its words. Jane Cornwell's
accompanying artwork, a standout among consistently excellent
illustrations, features a weather map overspread by isobars, with a heart
placed over her beloved Scotland.

'Call my eyes upward
to remember again,
there is an aqua sky'

A similar assuredness permeates *Call Me Home*, causing another
not entirely happy poem still to sink like a balm within the troubled
reader's soul. The light-footed rhythm and last stanza's slight refrain
serve to enhance the strong sense of musicality conjured up by Terrell's
words.

'I am content as distant windchimes
brush against my eardrum.'

Firmly into Summer now, the highly descriptive opening lines of
Dappled (On Impending Loss) anchor us in the bittersweetness of
borrowed time passed in the company of a loved one. By doing so,
they provide another poignant reminder of the inimitable value of the
present.

'For dormancy, though it may be dim, differs so from death.'

As *Decomposition* and *Seasons of Change* work their magic, the coldness
is settling in to *On the Wing* until we find ourselves lost *In Dark Shadows*,
where life seeks shelter and beats retreat, but the bugs still wriggle and
writhe beneath the surface.

'Perhaps, with reflection,
we can learn.'

As witnessed in 2023's *Confronting the Elements*, Terrell is a passionate, outspoken writer, deeply concerned by the footprint of recent human activity. These convictions come to the fore in *Collective Crisis* and *Let's Dance*, two poems interlinked in a similar manner to the blackbirds they portray, combining to juxtapose the *'cooperation, teamwork, and humility'* shown by the birds with the dog-eat-dog world of humankind, then imploring us to change for the better.

'We'll catch a glimpse of a bird on the wing,
and in its splendor, find ourselves accepting
we're all growing towards a moment.'

As both book and year draw to a close, *Behold* is a celebration of all things wondrous in nature, be they mysterious or entirely explainable, which gets one thinking maybe it is a child's eyes Terrell wants us to see through, that we may fully appreciate the beauty of living. In the magical closer, *Revelation*, we are again urged to look beyond dismissiveness and cynicism to see that in our present and sometimes prosaic seeming moments, there is poetry and music to be found; that a life *On the Wing* is a life spent in flight.

Lawrence Moore

To the fanciful and the grounded, the lovers of birds,
and the lovers of poetry. Thank you, dear readers. Be well~

CONTENTS

FOREWORD BY LAWRENCE MOORE   5

DEDICATION   9

REVERIE   12

DELICATE STRENGTH   14

DAYBREAK   15

A DAY   16

A NEW SONG   18

ANTICIPATING SPRING   19

SPRING RAIN   20

GOLD STAR DINER   21

UNFLAPPABLE   23

A STORM CALLED CUPID   25

FLIGHT UNDER PRESSURE   27

CALL ME HOME   28

CAUGHT EMPTY-HANDED   29

MAKE ME MAKE SENSE   30

ABSTRACTIONS   31

CROWS IN SUMMER   32

ADUMBRATION   34

MELTING	36
DAPPLED (ON IMPENDING LOSS)	37
SONG FOR MY SONS, LONG AFTER I'M GONE	38
DECOMPOSITION	40
SEASONS OF CHANGE	42
IN DARK SHADOWS	43
COLLECTIVE CRISIS	44
LET'S DANCE	45
CHRISTMAS CARDINALS	46
FLEDGLINGS	47
FROM WHENCE INSPIRATION COMES	48
BEHOLD	49
UNREACHABLE	50
SAFE LANDINGS	52
REVELATIONS	54
ACKNOWLEDGMENTS	56
SAMANTHA TERRELL	57
JANE'S STUDIO PRESS	58

REVERIE

For days, I've saved up whimsy in a jar,
like lightning bugs in summer.

Seashells, dragonflies, and colorful
beads, soprano notes and cornflowers

— all crowded
in together, busily swarming around,

occasionally glancing
out at the world as if to ask,

What comes next?
Of course, I'll release them

after sufficient observation,
before the oxygen

runs low; carefully stringing
beads onto the cornflower stem, or steadying

a seashell for a dragonfly perch, as the notes
of Debussy's "Reverie" float

gently away from here
to land softly in your ear.

DELICATE STRENGTH

Tailbone to tailbone in
fetal position, we
resemble butterfly wings.
Let's rest, and then
let's fly.

DAYBREAK

Fold yourself in half
each morning to
remember the gift of
who you are.
Bend instead of break
into the day.
Greet eternity
in the ache.
Light and birdsong
will follow.

A DAY

Discover me in
smiles and frequent glances.
Support me in
conversations, second chances.

Devour words that
call themselves my own.
My door opens,
to the unknown,

ushers out scarcity —
envelops the discovery
that is me — a day.
I'm the earth, where birds frolic and play;

Or, in your mind, consumed by reality's
stresses, discomforts *or* magnanimity.
All may be lost to time tomorrow,
but today owns every joy and sorrow.

A NEW SONG

A sleepless night and the monotony of the
latest top-of-the-charts plays itself
over and over and over.

Finally, enough. Spring beckons —
outside is a new song:

mating meadowlarks,
countless cardinals,
mourning doves, and more.

Life is made new
through music.

ANTICIPATING SPRING

It came on a whisper. The

Cat pawing quietly at the

door, a not-too-cool slither of
air seeping through;

Cracking barrier between
sight and taste;

The wait
to open
made worthwhile —

Licking lips, he saunters away,
determining a bird's song
mustn't be cut short, after all.

As though lips
could breathe
a season
into being.

SPRING RAIN

Finches flicker down from the great pagoda,
winged raindrops dripping to earth,

waking it with their words,
soaking the lawn in song.

GOLD STAR DINER

Lately, I eat lunch
with goldfinches.
They feed me with
their songs.
I offer them my silence.
I find the venue tasteful,
the fare — fair.
The fellowship?
Outstanding!

UNFLAPPABLE

We seem to have a wren nest
in our pansy basket,
nestled 'neath gold and purple petals.
Mama or Daddy flutters in, in a fury,
      settling frantic calls with a calming presence,

As a weak bloom drops to the floor, and
      grey skies offer thunder in reply.
For now, the frenzie's ended,
babies' needs have been attended.
Soon tiny wings, instead of storms, will greet the sky.

A STORM CALLED CUPID

Thou shalt be free
As mountain winds: but then exactly do
All points of my command.
- William Shakespeare, *The Tempest*

Shots from arrows pointed purposefully at hearts,
sometimes, get blocked.
The music of history gets in the way.
Its chaotic notes become temporarily jumbled.

A song in the air sounds off tune,
stirring up a storm for the ages.
Yet the arrow flies, despite gathering clouds
(they, too, fated for the sky).

Until the tempest and its aim,
both become stuck
in a bottle set to sea,
found by a lover, met by me.

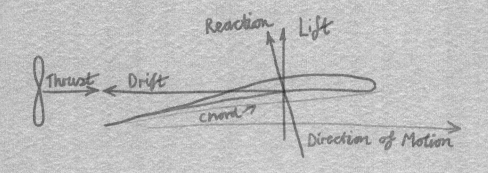

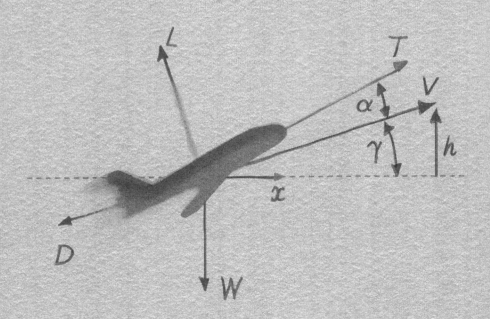

SAMANTHA TERRELL   ON THE WING

FLIGHT UNDER PRESSURE

Pacing, mind racing,
stress and caffeine taking their toll —
questions and fears appear
at every mental turn —
too few options,
too much time?

As deadlines and policy,
procedures and expectations,
oversight and standards
loom, and complaints, questions,
problems,
relentlessly urge for attention,

another mental puzzle
presents itself:
When clouds
close in towards tree-tops, and
the trees press upward
towards the storm,

where does the bird go for refuge?

CALL ME HOME

Call me home,
beyond the graveyard
of self-defeat,
beyond the unkempt,
cracked, and
callous-producing street,

to that place before weary
where I never wept,
nor feared
for all the empty soda-can
brokenness and disgrace of
this world's countless years.

Call my eyes upward
to remember again,
there is an aqua sky
way up above the hurt and
useless junk, where American
eagles still take flight.

CAUGHT EMPTY-HANDED

Blank mind spaces
make compelling cases

for right or wrong; known or unknown;
lost or found; foreign lands or home.

But a desire to fly
doesn't make the dream take to sky.

Reveling in too little, leaves too much air of ambiguity.
Reaching too far for fullness, results in handfuls of empty.

MAKE ME MAKE SENSE

A heart needs to *thump-bump, thump-bump,*
not just one or the other, to make a thing live.
A mockingbird in a world void of sound
searches in vain for a talent that's elusive.

A rose bush that has
not one bloom
is but a sticker-bush,
even in sunny June.

So a heart may go '*thump-bump*'
just fine, throughout each season.
But this life without truth,
is a life without reason.

ABSTRACTIONS

Making sense of mossy
abstract greys and greens,
the eyes of the mind see
a proliferation of vegetation,
as hen and chicks begin again
in repurposed terrariums

from some old Mother's Day —
signifying children and growth;
elders and death;
soil and botany.
Abstract greys and greens
are life-force, made concrete.

CROWS IN SUMMER

Our neighborhood murder is back.
It makes me smile.

They strut their laps
across our lawns,

teaching their young to peck in grass,
forage for grubs, and such.

I watch through the fog.
They probably see me anyway.

Even in the relaxed ways of summer,
a parent is always watching.

ADUMBRATION

Queen Anne's Lace and black crows
frame my mental imagery,
succumbing to the picture's Rule of Thirds until,
there's only room to run off the page,

though white cobwebs remain in corners,
darkness marches from the recesses of my mind,
as a murmuration of starlings in flight, not unlike
a militaristic Rule of Thirds deployment.

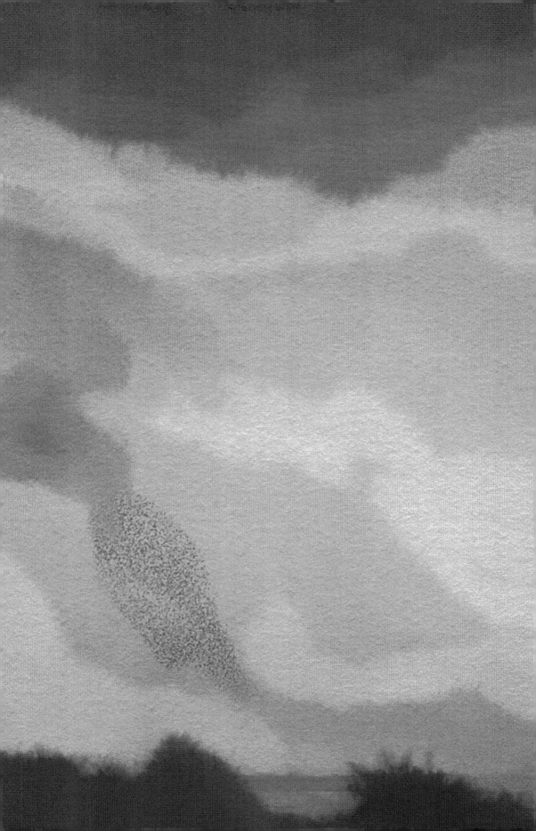

MELTING

Tonight features a flame of
upswept clouds reaching
beyond flying fowl, to
lick the dome of ice cream sky,

melting from under us —
Drip, drip, dripping —
puddles become floods.

Drip, drip, dripping —
becomes weeping
as reasonable-minded
people, everywhere, cry.

DAPPLED (ON IMPENDING LOSS)

Today is sunshine and birds singing and
mowers buzzing around the neighborhood.

And, I am content as distant windchimes
brush against my eardrum.

Even an aggressive dog barking and a
horn honking aren't bothersome.

But, today is good on the back
of the bad;

held up by the fact, you take a part of us
with you when you go.

So, we are here, in scattered sunlight patches,
breathing in fresh-cut grass —

and, not here — waiting for
shadows and dank to overtake us.

Knowing there are some problems
we can't think ourselves out of,

we wait for the heart to
love us out of them, instead.

SONG FOR MY SONS, LONG AFTER I'M GONE

Tell me you whistle back at the noisy birds
in the neighborhood.
      whoo-wee, whoo-wee

Do you pick up the occasional rock with interesting pock-
marks, when your interest is piqued?

Please, assure me you smile back at
the baby in the supermarket basket,

or help the elderly
collect an item gone astray.

Because times will come (if they haven't already),
when pain creates an eddy

like a closed-circuit pathway
in your heart's brain.

And, when they come, please also, let them go;
pierce the stream; find a way through the sorrow.

On second thought, you don't have to tell me, if you know
      the delight of meeting a stranger's grateful smile,
after riding that painful current for awhile.

I must trust you'll discover (if you haven't already), that
      doing all in your power
to ensure happiness in another,

is the purest pleasure worth finding.
So, in wanting it for you, forgive me my reminding.

DECOMPOSITION

Winter birds have yet to
beckon at the bird feeder door,
and leaf litter hasn't yet
been tracked in upon the floor.

But summertime is waning.
Down deep, I feel
days stretching (lengthwise, vertical, diagonal);
        pulling apart; decomposing —
the way of nature after weeks and weeks

exposed, when sun and
summer wind
have won their battles,
wearing all things thin.

SEASONS OF CHANGE

Apple cider spills
over into
egg-nog season,

as barren branches fill
with chickadees,
instead of leaves.

Grey skies promise the thrill
of snow.
But I refuse to believe.

IN DARK SHADOWS

Empty silhouettes of life waiting
      calmly in their steadfast way,
tucked far from the sun's rays
can reach the dark forest floor,
as moss creeps quietly beneath the stalwart trees
      beyond the woodland's door.

And birds have hushed their calls,
as winter demands its annual stall.
Creeping things, too, though they still creep,
do so more deeply. But the shadowed woods are full of dens and nests,
      where foxes and fowl sleep.

For dormancy, though it may be dim, differs so from death.

COLLECTIVE CRISIS

Blackbirds swarm overhead, a
chaotic mass of synchronicity in motion,
their internal radars
feeding off one another.

But, movement
is not
equal to
progress.

We are blackbirds,
forcing motion upon
each other in tugging,
pushing, pulling masses,

always making time for arguing over direction —
never making enough time to recognize
our self-created, collective crisis of ignorance
married to arrogance.

No, we are not blackbirds, after all, with
their cooperation, teamwork, and humility.
Perhaps, with reflection,
we can learn.

LET'S DANCE

Clusters of blackbirds
dance across the
late December sky —
notes on a page in
singular rhythm,
bringing order to the
expansive canvas above.
Unaware, unthreatened
by the boldness they display,
selflessly working together
proficiently, in solidarity
against a stark contrast of vast
unrestrained immenseness —
urging all of nature to
Do the same, do the same, do the SA-AME?

CHRISTMAS CARDINALS

We rounded the corner
and they appeared —
untameable treasures to behold, a simple yet
astounding sight. A flash of red,
a grey-brown flutter,
and the flock of beauty scattered
harmlessly before us, escalating gracefully
into naked branches stretching up silently
into shadows. From nowhere, the immaterial became incarnate
in our very presence — the ultimate gift.

FLEDGLINGS

The unlikely, top heavy, more showy
than functionally-equipped, can still learn to fly.

The supervision of such a learning endeavor
(potentially burdensome beyond measure),

weighs down the wings of both apprentice and mentor,
but proves the value of work required to soar.

FROM WHENCE INSPIRATION COMES

Northwest windswept wishes

blow through barren notebooks,

blank pages, empty dreams

until the cold and desolate that foretold only doom,

is met with fresh sentiments on an updraft from

some summer far away.

BEHOLD

So what, if fire isn't magic after all? And, as it turns out,
        fog is simply condensed water particles.

Yes, there's a scientific explanation for an eagle in flight,
        the age of fossils, translucence of leaves in sunshine.

Aren't they all still miracles, anyway?

UNREACHABLE

I stand in a valley
watching birds I cannot touch,
meditating on their songs — great compositions
that seem to know no end.

Forced into a stillness I did not select,
I find the wings of my worries
mysteriously fluttering off with the birds —
their presence, a comfort absent of closure.

SAFE LANDINGS

When the great eternal gavel drops,
let it be known
I found the sunset
stunning from the start,
and always trusted
in the purity of your heart.

Before its head is turned and laid to rest,
tell the Judge of your anger,
your cloud full of tears,
life's bliss, your heart's motivation,
death's wretched fears,
and even depression.
And when it falls
with its mighty thud,
we'll stand together, accepting and accepted
in those grand immortal halls.

REVELATIONS

Let's wander until we find the moon
lingering in the morning fog
cliché. Perhaps if we go there

we'll finally find out we're exactly who
we were always accused of being.
It will be simultaneously disappointing

and
revelatory.
Then we can continue our stories.

We're all growing towards a moment.
Its largesse can be intimidating.
Maybe by admitting

the moon lingering in the morning fog
can never truly be reduced to cliché —
we'll be okay.

ACKNOWLEDGMENTS

Personal acknowledgments:

First, I wish to extend my gratitude to Paul Brookes of *The Wombwell Rainbow* for the poetry prompts and support which inspired some of the poems in this chapbook, and Jane Cornwell for her amazing publishing support and beautiful illustrations. I consider myself blessed to have met and collaborated with both Paul and Jane on multiple projects. As always, I'd also like to thank my family for their continual encouragement, which sustains me through the ups and downs of the writing business and life itself!

Professional acknowledgments:

In addition, first publish credits and my heartfelt gratitude are due to the following presses or publications where these poems first appeared, sometimes in a different form:

A Day (*The Organic Poet*)
A Storm Called Cupid (*Skyway Journal*)
Collective Crisis (*Reverie*)
Decomposition (*Wildfire Words*)
From Whence Inspiration Comes (*Door Is A Jar*)
Revelations (*Critical Muslim*)
Safe Landings (*A Thin Slice of Anxiety*).

SAMANTHA TERRELL

Samantha Terrell is a Pushcart-nominated poet and the author of multiple collections, most recently *Dismantling Mountains* (Vellum Publishing UK, 2023). Her poems have been widely anthologized in publications such as *Dark Winter Lit, Green Ink Poetry, In Parentheses, Misfit Magazine, Open Journal of Arts & Letters, Poetry Quarterly, Red Weather, Wildfire Words*, and others. Terrell writes from Upstate New York where she lives with her husband, two teenagers, two cats, a dog, and a growing collection of over-watered houseplants.

Jane Cornwell is an artist, illustrator and book designer. After responding to Paul Brookes call out for an artist to provide 30 prompt artworks for a National Poetry Month Ekphrastic Challenge, 2020, she discovered that she really enjoys reading and listening to poetry. She realised she could give some deserving poets the chance to get their work published and set up her own small poetry press, Jane's Studio Press. Since, she's collaborated with Paul Brookes, Samantha Terrell, Susan Richardson and Lawrence Moore to create poetry books. Committing to producing these books in her free time means Jane has to keep her drawing and painting skills up, and she enjoys working in a collaborative way with her chosen poets.

Jane has exhibited with the RSW at the National Gallery of Scotland, The Big Art Show, Glasgow, SSA, Knock Castle Gallery, Aberdeen Artists Society, The Glasgow Group, Paisley Art Institute, MacMillan Exhibition at Bonhams, Edinburgh, The House For An Art Lover, Pittenweem Arts Festival, Compass Gallery, The Revive Show, East Linton Art Exhibition and Strathkelvin Annual Art Exhibition.

Jane is a member of Publishing Scotland and the Association of Illustrators. She graduated with a BA(Hons) in Design from the Glasgow School of Art, age 20.

Her website is: www.janecornwell.co.uk.

Made in the USA
Columbia, SC
09 September 2024

41457582R00033